All right reserved. No part of this publication may be reproduced, distributed or transmitted in any form or by any means, including photocopying, recording, other electronic or mechanical methods without prior written permission of the publisher except in case of brief quotation embodied in critical reviews and certain noncommercial use permitted by copyright law.

Contents

Pet Sitting for Profit by Patti Moran 4
Pet Sitting 5
Ideas for Starting a Pet Business 7
Is a Pet Business the Right Business for you? 20
Professional Pet Sitter Job Description Template 22
Pet Sitter Job Summary 23
Job Responsibilities 24
Job Skills & Qualifications 26
Pet Sitter Job Responsibilities 27
Pet Sitter Job Specifications 29
Ways to Keep your Pet-Sitting Business Successful in Any Economy 31
What Keeps your Pet-Sitting Business Successful? 37
Is Pet Business Profitable? 38
Pet Business Ideas & Opportunities 39
Frequently Asked Questions on Pet Business 58

Benefits of Using Pet Sitting Service..60

Difference between a Professional Pet Sitter and a Hobby Pet Sitter..65

Professional Pet Sitters...67

Where Can I Find a Certified Professional Pet Sitter?................71

National Association of Professional Pet Sitters (NAPPS)..........73

Benefits of Pet Sitting Over Pet Boarding..................................74

Pet Sitting Insurance Policy Information...................................76

What Does Pet Sitting Insurance Cover?...................................83

Pet Sitting for Profit by Godfrey Babs

What is the economic situation in your area? Are there neighborhoods of affluence, middle class, or lower income? You probably already know that money doesn't make a person a better pet owner, so while it's tempting to only market to those with plenty of it, don't ignore the middle or lower income residents. They may not be able to afford premium or unnecessary services (like dog walking when they are at home, for example) but they still need care when they are out of town or unable to do tasks like giving medication to their pets.

Market research and networking

Ask around and learn what people do for pet care in your area. Do they exchange with friends or neighbors, hire a professional, or use an app-based service? How many other pet sitters are in the area? A Google search of "pet sitter near me" will show you sitters with established websites in your area. A search on Rover.com will show you how many individuals advertise services through the app.

Pick up the phone and call the other sitters to see if they want to meet. Pet sitting is a lonely business, and most sitters are friendly and open. There may already be a networking group in your area, so find out how you can join. I have been happy to mentor a number of new sitters over the years, and I made lifelong friends doing so.

Pet Sitting

Pet sitting makes the top of the list because there's nearly a universal need for it and it's a very flexible business. For instance, if you live in a suitable place out of town, you can run a pet sitting business as a kennel operation with people bringing their pets to you and dropping them off.

But you can also go to people's homes and look after their pets' needs. Or you can combine a pet-sitting business with a house-sitting business and look after everything while your customers are away. Retirees, in particular, tend to travel regularly, making pet and house sitting a popular business for catering to seniors.

Ideas for Starting a Pet Business

A Growing Opportunity

According to the American Pet Products Association:

- 67% of U.S. households own at least one pet.
- Approximately 89.7 million dogs, 94.2 million cats, and 139.3 million freshwater fish were owned in the United States in 2017-2018 (the three largest categories of pets).
- Americans spent $72.56 billion on their pets in 2018, up from $69.51 billion in 2017. This number has been rising steadily since 1994.

The pet services segment, including grooming, boarding, pet hotels, pet sitting, day care and other services, has been the fastest-growing category; Americans spent $6.11 billion on pet services in 2018 and this figure is expected to rise to over 6$.31 billion in 2019.

In Canada, households spent $8.85 billion on pets in 2018, according to Statistics Canada. Another study showed that around 41% of households have at least one dog, and 38% of households own at least one cat. Internationally, China is experiencing compound annual growth rates in pet ownership of more than 7%.

The ideas below range from pet-based products to providing pet services that involve working with animals, but you won't find any pet business ideas on the list that involve the retail breeding and selling of animals. Both the American and Canadian Societies for the Prevention of Cruelty to Animals are opposed to this practice.

Pet Sitting

Pet sitting makes the top of the list because there's nearly a universal need for it and it's a very flexible business. For instance, if you live in a suitable place out of town, you can run a pet sitting business as a kennel operation with people bringing their pets to you and dropping them off.

But you can also go to people's homes and look after their pets' needs. Or you can combine a pet-sitting business with a house-sitting business and look after everything while your customers are away. Retirees, in particular, tend to travel regularly, making pet and house sitting a popular business for catering to seniors.

Pet Boarding

This is a riff on the pet-sitting business idea, where you have a facility set up where dogs and cats can be dropped off and looked after while their owners are gone. The main challenge with this model is zoning. You may not be able to do it where you are, so be sure you check your local bylaws and zoning restrictions first.

Doggie Day Care

Another pet business idea on the same theme, the doggie day care has very similar pros and cons. There is an increasing need for this kind of pet service as more working people are discovering that dogs left alone day after day while the owner works can bark and be destructive. On the downside, though, you may find this a difficult business to locate because of zoning regulations and municipal bylaws.

Dog Training

If you can offer dog obedience training and it well—you can probably write your own ticket. There are an awful lot of people out there who don't have enough time or skill (or either one) to train a dog properly but for some reason, they've bought one anyway and now need someone to train it. The venue is not necessarily a problem; facilities to run dog training classes can be rented.

Pet Training

If you're a skilled animal trainer and have an interest in media, a pet business specializing in training animals for film and TV may be for you. Remember Morris the cat? Lobo? Moose, the Jack Russell Terrier on the TV show Frasier? Some animals become huge stars. Hollywood Paws (based in Los Angeles) is an example of a business that trains animals and their owners to work in the entertainment industry.

Pet-Finding Business

Are you the kind of person who enjoys solving puzzles? Maybe you've even thought of being a detective at some point. If so, you might put your sleuthing skills to work running a pet-finding business. You can help distraught pet owners get their loved ones back and make money while you're at it. Pure Gold Pet Trackers is one example of a business that uses the tracking skills of Golden Retrievers to find lost pets.

Dog Walking

Another dog-related service that busy pet owners need is to have their dogs walked regularly. The key to success with this pet business idea is time management. You'd definitely want to have enough clients in close proximity so you could take a number of dogs out for a walk at once, rather than cycling through them one at a time.

Dog Grooming

Dog grooming is a popular pet business, since grooming is one of those chores of dog ownership that many would rather pay someone else to do than do themselves. Another reason for its popularity is that, like pet sitting, it's quite a flexible business concept. You could operate a dog grooming business as a mobile service or run it out of a retail shop, for example.

Pooper Scooper

While we're on the subject of chores related to dog ownership that people would rather avoid, don't forget poop scooping. This involves visiting customers' properties on a weekly or monthly basis and collecting and disposing of dog feces.

Yes, it's dirty, messy work, but so are lots of things that people do to make money. On the plus side, there's no special training or equipment needed and you can easily operate this business from home.

Dog Bathing

Having bathed dogs before, I can definitely see why some people don't want to do this in their own homes. Wet and messy only begins to describe it. A dog-bathing business could be operated as a standalone business or as an adjunct to a pet-grooming business. Or you could run this as a do-it-yourself business, where all you provide are the facilities and the equipment.

Pet Massage Therapy

So far I've written about pet services related to pets' basic needs. But there's a whole growing sector of pet businesses related to their not-so-basic needs, as pet owners look for more ways to help their pets lead longer and healthier lives. Pet massage services are one of these niche markets that seem to be growing. Iâ€™ve also seen pet businesses offering acupuncture, hydrotherapy, and even psychotherapy. In many of these fields, there is specific pet-related training required to become a practitioner.

Pet Restaurant

And speaking of upscale pet services, what about restaurants devoted to dogs? No, not just restaurants that allow you to bring dogs with you, but restaurants where the dogs are the diners. Is this a pet business that would be allowed where you are? You'd definitely need to check both health regulations and municipal bylaws before moving forward.

Pet Food

Just as with the food they put into their own bodies, pet owners have become increasingly concerned about the quality of the food their pets eat. People are continually on the lookout for pet foods that they feel have additional health benefits. There are basically two approaches to pet food businesses: You can either produce the pet food yourself or become a distributor for a particular type of food. Dog bakeries, homemade healthy dog treats, raw foods, gourmet foods any of these could be extremely lucrative if the pets (and the owners) like what's on offer.

Pooch Couture

Pets or children? The difference between them has blurred considerably in the eyes of many pet owners. Many dog owners like to dress up their pets, which creates all kinds of pet business opportunities to supply dogs with fashionable, good-looking gear. (Cat owners know that they'll be lucky to get away with putting a collar, let alone anything else, on little Tiger, so the opportunities for creating and selling cat gear are much more limited.) Once again, you can create the couture yourself or distribute someone else's.

Pet-Supply Store

All kinds of pets need supplies and gear, and pet owners seem to like the convenience of being able to "one-stop shop". This kind of pet business seems to be dominated by franchises, but it is still possible to start your own company from scratch. Such a business could also supply pet-related services as well, such as dog grooming. Picture an in-house "dog spa," for example, surrounded by products for sale.

Pet-Business Marketing

The key to success for many small businesses is to find and fill a niche market. Pet-business marketing is an example of this. There are so many pet businesses now that it's possible to run a successful marketing business that caters to the needs of pet-business owners exclusively. FWV Fetching, for instance, provides everything from blogging placement and social media to trade show campaigns exclusively for pet businesses. If you have the marketing expertise, pet marketing might be the business you've been looking for.

Pet-Portrait Business

If you have artistic talent and love animals, you might start a business painting portraits of people's pets. Along these same lines, you might start a pet photography business if that's where your talents lie. You'll probably need a lot of patience during the sittings required when you're working to portray an animal, though. Be that as it may, as people give their pets greater importance in their lives, they seem to have an increasing need to commemorate them.

Veterinarian

Being a veterinarian is the original pet business. And nowadays, veterinarians are able to make good livings specializing in treating pets of all kinds. The downside is that this is a business that requires years of training and, like being a human doctor, has strict accreditation and licensing requirements.

Is a Pet Business the Right Business for you?

To run a successful pet business, you have to love and be knowledgeable about the animals you're going to work with, and, as you see from the descriptions of the businesses above, that can sometimes involve years of specialized training.

But you also have to bear in mind that even that isn't enough. A pet business is just like any other small business; the key to success is choosing the right business for the right time and place. You may be a wonderful dog groomer, but if you live in a small town and there are already three dog grooming businesses operating there, you're going to have a tough time of it.

Before you start a pet business, do the research and work through a business plan, just as you would for any new business venture. The planning process is an important step in determining if your pet business idea will be a success.

Professional Pet Sitter Job Description Template

A pet sitter is responsible for caring for pets when their owners are not available. A sitter may groom, feed and exercise pets. Pet sitters may work based upon a set schedule or provide services on a periodic basis when the owner is unable to do so. Some sitters may also offer training services.

As you create a pet sitter job description, you want to emphasize that a pet sitter must be familiar with and able to work with pets of all kinds. They should be trustworthy because they may be given access to customers' homes. Sitters should also be physically able to exercise and care for pets.

A pet sitter needs to have a great love for animals, along with being friendly and possessing customer service skills. Look at the following example to help you get an idea of how to construct your own pet sitter job description.

Pet Sitter Job Summary

Do you love animals? You may be perfect for our current pet sitter job opening. We are looking for someone who wants to help owners provide the highest level of care for their pets when they can't do it themselves. You should have experience working with animals and knowledgeable about the general needs of dogs, cats and small rodents. You will be responsible for offering general care for a range of animals, along with walking and cleaning up after dogs of every breed and size. You should love the outdoors and enjoy playing with pets who are energetic. Our pet sitting service strives to provide high-level care while offering our employees a flexible schedule and great benefits, which include health care, bonuses and paid vacations.

Job Responsibilities

- Clean up after, groom, exercise and provide care for cats, dogs and small rodents, includes dog walking services and litter box and cage cleaning
- Observe outdoor and indoor play to ensure safety of the pet

- Feed and provide water based upon client instructions, which may be very detailed and must be followed exactly as given
- Meet with potential clients to secure business, advertise services provided and explain the details of how pet sitting works
- Report any injuries or illnesses to manager as soon as possible, along with completing an injury/illness form to turn in as soon as manager is on-site
- Respect clients' homes and personal property when on-site offering pet sitting services, includes cleaning up any pet messes
- Provide additional customer service as requested by clients, which may include picking up mail, watering plants and opening and closing blinds or curtains
- Check and follow schedule provided by the main office and report any conflicts or issues to manager as soon as possible but at least 24 hours in advance of scheduled sitting appointment

Job Skills & Qualifications

Required

- Must love animals
- Be at least 18 years old
- Have a reliable vehicle and valid driver's license
- Pass criminal background check
- Ability to work varying schedules

Preferred:

- Previous experience working with animals, especially large dog breeds
- Ability to work overnight hours, weekends and holidays
- Want to use this job description?

Pet Sitter Job Responsibilities

An accurate list of job responsibilities will do a lot for your pet sitter job description. When done well, the job responsibilities section can communicate the shape of the role in a way that funnels well-suited candidates your way, while helping less appropriate jobseekers save themselves and you from wasting their time with an application.

- Be sure to pare down your list to 6-8 core items for maximum impact; save less central pet sitter job responsibilities to

explain during later parts of the hiring process. This is a great place to establish the types of animals that your new hire will care for.
- If you're having trouble getting started on your pet sitter job description, consider modeling your responsibilities on the following examples:

- Travel to customers homes and visit with their cats, dogs, birds or other pets
- Feed and water pets according to customer instructions regarding preparation, quantity and time of day
- Exercise pets with leashed walks and/or play
- Administer supplements and/or medications to pets in food or otherwise
- Collect and dispose of pet waste (cleaning/refreshing kitty litter for cats, changing cage paper for birds, picking up waste on walks with dogs, etc.)

- Document pet care with dates, times and services rendered in a neat and professional manner

Pet Sitter Job Specifications

The job qualifications and skills section of a pet sitter job description may be difficult to put together. Experience can be a muddy subject when it comes to pet sitting, and education generally isn't required.

So what does belong in a great set of pet sitter job specifications? Some experience is needed, of course. Consider whether you'd accept sporadic care for relatives or roommates pets or a history of pet ownership or other indirect types of experiences with animals. Then clearly lay out your minimum requirements. Often pet sitters must have a personal vehicle" it may be a good idea to include this in your specifications if that is the case. You may also wish to specify availability requirements. Other than that, consider what soft skills or attributes you'd like to see in candidates: reliability, love of animals, and a detail-oriented nature are all common desired qualities in pet sitters.

Here are some examples you can tweak to fit the specific role of your own pet sitter job description:

- Must passionately care for animals of all types
- Must demonstrate history of reliability; must also pass a basic background check
- Experience in pet care required (pet ownership and previous pet sitting experience are both acceptable); experience with both dogs and cats preferred

- Must be available weekends and holidays as needed
- Required ability to follow detailed instructions to the letter
- Must have access to reliable transportation for home visits
- Making better hires starts with building better job descriptions

Ways to Keep your Pet-Sitting Business Successful in Any Economy

Continued economic challenges, combined with an influx of "hobbyist pet sitters" advertising online, are causing many pet sitters to stress over the impact it will have on business. Fortunately, spending on pets remains high, the need for pet-sitting services continues to grow, and by taking a few extra precautions, professional pet sitters can ensure their pet-sitting business remains the #1 choice for local pet owners.

To maintain the success of your pet-sitting business:

1. Diversify your services. Pet owners have many different needs. If the economy has caused a decrease in your pet-sitting assignments, consider other services that may benefit your existing and potential clients. Consider offering overnights, daily dog walks or pet taxi services, to name a few.

It's also important to understand that pet sitting isn't simply for dogs and cats anymore. In fact, arecent report from market research firm Packaged Facts says there are 116 million fish, birds, small mammals, reptiles and other such pets, including 7.2 million households with fish tanks, 4.6 million with bird cages and 1.8 million with reptiles. There are also 2.5 million adults who own rabbits. Are you effectively advertising your services to these pet owners and do you have the necessary pet-care knowledge to offer these services? If not, it's the perfect time to learn. Explore PSI's online courses, speak with friends or family members who own these types of pets and seek out volunteer opportunities with pet-rescue groups or facilities that specialize in particular species to increase your knowledge and experience.

2. Re-examine your service area. While it is tempting to take any and every pet-sitting assignment—especially if business has been slow consider your overhead costs. Traveling outside of your immediate service area costs additional money and time and offers little to no profit. Consider revising your service area, or charging a mileage fee for clients outside of a specific range. Focus marketing efforts on convenient neighborhoods that have proven to offer the largest clientele.

Another option is to hire staff sitters to handle these other assignments. If you decide to expand your pet-sitting staff, you'll need to decide if you should hire employees or work with independent contractors. You'll also need to determine the best way to locate and identify the best sitters for your business.

Also, always remember that it is okay to say no to a pet-sitting assignment, even if it is in your service area, if you feel uncomfortable. Pet sitters report that there are four main reasons they turn down pet-sitting assignments and it's important to always listen to your gut.

3. Broaden your (marketing) horizons. E-mail and Internet marketing campaigns offer simple "and often free "ways to reach current and potential clients. Step outside of your comfort zone andconsider trying social media, such as blogs, Facebook, YouTube or Twitter to promote your business to local pet owners.

Online advertising options are great, but don't forget the power of word-of-mouth recommendations. Make it easy for your pet-sitting clients to spread the word about your services. Give them referral cards to share with their friends or family and consider offering a one-time discount to clients who refer new clients.

4. Maintain excellent service. Spending less time at a visit or forgoing leaving a daily note may allow you to fit more visits in a day, but decreased service is never a good idea"in any economy. By continuing to offer stellar care and possibly even adding benefits, such as new client referral rewards, you are sure to outlast any economic downturn or increased influx of pet-sitting services in your area. It's also important to make sure your pet-sitting clients know what excellent service you are providing. Keep them informed about what you do for them and the standards to which you conform. Leave checklists and "report cards" after each pet-sitting assignment. Thank your customer with handwritten notes, e-mails and calls. Finally, ask them how you can improve,

realign and expand your services to help them even more.

5. Network, Network, Network! The importance of networking can never be stressed enough. Involvement in a local pet-sitting network or networking with fellow pet sitters online through PSI's Member Forum or in person at our annual Quest for Excellence convention is a great way to receive support, advice and referrals. A strong professional network is essential for success, regardless of the state of the economy.

You never know who could refer a new client, so don't just limit your networking to pet-industry professionals. Many pet sitters report great client referrals from hair-salon owners, employees at medical facilities, travel agents, law enforcement and bank tellers.

Recently, PSI pet sitter Pocono Pet Nanny got excellent exposure through a television commercial that came about from doing something we all do "buying and getting her car serviced at her local vehicle dealership. You never know who can help spread the word about your pet-sitting services!

What Keeps your Pet-Sitting Business Successful?

With pet ownership on the rise, the pet-sitting industry continues to grow. It's important for new pet sitters to establish a strong foundation for their business. For established professional pet sitters wanting to maintain or grow their businesses, it's necessary to understand the mindset and routines of local pet owners and create a service package that meets their pet-care needs.

Has your pet-sitting business had to grow or adapt to remain successful in the current market? What are you doing differently now than you did five years ago to ensure that you continue to keep your current pet-sitting clients happy"and gain new clients?

Is Pet Business Profitable?

The pet industry is growing rapidly worldwide. People are buying more pets nowadays and spending a lot of money on them to give the ultimate comfort. The attitude and sentiment behind this are the majority of the population now considers their pet to be a member of the family.

According to the market study, freshwater fish, cats, dogs, birds, reptiles, horses and saltwater fishes are the most popular pet globally. Market research company WSL indicates that 81% of respondents are spending the same amount or more on their pets despite the tough economic times.

Pet Business Ideas & Opportunities

Open a One-Stop Pet Shop

Opening a pet shop is a lucrative pet-related business idea. Most attractive retail opportunities for pet lovers. Either you can start with a franchise or of your own.

Pet Breeding Business

There is no shortage of customers to buy pets all across the world. Additionally, the profit margin of selling pets is also high. If you are a pet lover and want to make money money, the pet breeding business is an extremely profitable business venture.

Pet Cremation Services

Pet cremation is another profitable and rewarding pet-related business. Most pet owners find it challenging to organize a proper funeral for their pets. Industry experts predict a huge growth of the pet funeral industry in the coming years.

Pet Cage Making

You can start a pet cage-making business from home. Knowledge and expertise are the basic criteria to get into the business. People like good-looking cages with effective interiors.

Cat Breeding & Selling

Cats are friendly pets to have around. Cats breed very fast. Car breeding and selling from home are some of the best pet-related business ideas around the world.

Dog Breeding Business

Dog owners are very conscious of the quality breed. It's a million-dollar industry nowadays.

Maintaining pedigrees is a must in the dog breeding business.

Dog Clothes Manufacturing

Dog clothes are very popular. The demand is high in cold climatic zones. You can start a dog clothing manufacturing business from home. Very little capital is required to start this pet business.

Dog Day Care Service

Dog daycare service is a profitable pet-related business. The market is huge. The service is also very popular among pet owners. Dogs are social creatures and need contact with people and other dogs to become well-behaved and confident. Dog daycare is strictly a drop-off in the morning and pick-up in the evening or anytime during the day type of operation.

Dog Obedience Training

Dog obedience training classes can be held at your home in a one-on-one or group format. You can also deal with schools and community centers to hold dog obedience classes on weekends and nights.

Dog Training for Hunting

Training dogs for hunting purposes is a good opportunity to earn money. Right knowledge and skill are required in this business.

Dog Training For Security

A trained dog can do a lot when it comes to securing lives and properties. Individual pet owners and security companies both can be your client.

Dog Walking Service

A dog walking service is perfectly suited for a dog lover who has the time and patience. There are various styles of multi-lead dog walking collars and leashes available that will allow three or more dogs to be walked at the same time without becoming tangled in the leash.

Guard Dog Security Service

Providing a guard dog security service is a very profitable business. Trained guard dogs are useful in airports, seaports, event venues, etc.

Kennel Cleaning Service

You can start this business of your own. Otherwise, you can do the marketing of this business for others.

Manicurist

For pet owners who don't want to go through the hassle of trimming their dogs' or cats' nails, they want to hire a pet manicurist. Some may even pay you to paint their pets' nails.

Mobile Pet Clinic

In a mobile pet clinic, you require a vehicle. You must be well equipped with emergency medicines and instruments.

Mobile Pet Grooming Business

Mobile pet grooming is getting popular among customers. Right skill and experience are required. Put emphasis on marketing aspects.

Aquarium Maintenance

In the aquarium maintenance business, the primary services are cleaning and maintaining your client's aquarium. It is a wonderful business for pet lovers. Selling allied products like food, colors, decor items will give you an extra margin.

You can also sell tropical fishes with this business. Make business tie-ups with interior designers.

Online Pet Accessories Selling

The Pet accessories market is increasing rapidly. Perfect pet-related business for people who have knowledge about current trends. You can sell through marketplaces like eBay. Otherwise, you can start your own online store.

Organic Pet Food Selling

The organic pet food market is increasing very fast. Sourcing is a vital factor in the success of this business. You can also sell these products from online marketplaces.

Organize Pet Competitions

Pet competition involves pet owners coming out with their pets to compete with other pets. You can also earn money from advertisement revenues.

Pet Accessories Manufacturing

This is a profitable business. It requires knowledge about technology and current trends. You need to invest sufficient cash investment to start this business.

Pet Adoption Business

It is a business that keeps pets that are rescued and also a business that gives people the opportunity to adopt any pet of their choice from pet homes. One of the coolest pet-related business ideas to start with no money

Pet Blogging

Have sound knowledge about pets? Pet blogging is one of the most profitable pet-related business ideas for you. Furthermore, besides consulting, you can earn through selling products from your blog.

Pet Body Care Products Manufacturing

Shampoo, soap, cream, lotions are popular pet body care products. The manufacturing of these products is a profitable venture. Substantial capital investment is required.

Pet Boutique

One of the most profitable pet-related business ideas in the retail industry. Start the store in a high traffic zone. Promote the store locally.

Pet Cemetery Business

Operating a pet cemetery is all about providing a burial ground for pet owners. This type of business is rapidly growing in developed countries.

Pet Coffins Selling

Making and selling coffins for a pet is a profitable business. Local promotion is required in this business. Start from home with small capital.

Pet Drugs Manufacturing

The Pet drug market is growing rapidly. Pet drug manufacturing is a profitable business. Experience in pharmaceuticals is a must.

Pet Dying Specialist

People dye their hair all the time. Some pet owners like adding different colors to their animals' fur. You can start this business as home-based.

Pet Food Production

Pet food is a daily necessity for pet owners. Foods for dogs, cats, birds, and fishes are the most popular. Pet food production is a capital-intensive business.

Pet House Making

Most pet owners look for a decorative house for their pets. They also look for furniture like beds etc. Very profitable business. You can start with limited capital investment.

Pet Insurance Company Business

Pet owners who truly love and cherish their pets pay a huge amount of cash to ensure their pets. It requires an insurance license from the organization regulating the insurance industry.

Pet Lodging Business

Pet lodges are places where pet owners keep their pets for professionals to help them take care of their pets when they are not going to be in town for a period of time. Start the business as home-based.

Pet Marketing eCommerce

A niche eCommerce for pets is one of the most profitable pet-related business ideas. It requires capital for promotion.

Pet Massage Therapy

Massages have been shown to benefit cats, dogs, and various other animals. With the right knowledge, you can offer your services as a pet massage therapist.

Pet Movie Producing

You can produce movies on pets. Most adorable entertainments for pet lovers. The advertisement revenue potential is very lucrative.

Pet Photography

The business of pet photography is ideal for pet lovers with artistic talent. Pet owners can be your clients. Else, you can sell photographs online.

Pet Related Radio Talk Show

A well-organized radio talk show to address key issues as it relates to pets and useful tips for handling pets is very good business. You will surely attract a large listenership and, of course, mouthwatering sponsorship deals from corporate pet businesses.

Pet Related TV Show

Pet-related TV shows are popular among pet lovers. You can earn very good advertisement revenue out of it.

Pet Sitting Business

Many people prefer to have their dogs, cats, and other pets for the safety and familiar surroundings of home, rather than an unfamiliar boarding environment. When these pet owners want or need to be away from their homes, there is only one solution available: hire a pet-sitting service to come to their homes and take care of their beloved pets while they're away.

Pet Spa Operator

There is a plenty of different health and beauty type of services you can offer for animals. Else you could offer a more all-encompassing spa experience for pets.

Pet Tag Engraver

Pet owners often want tags for their petsâ€™ collars. It gives their name and contact information. So you could allow customers to order custom pet tags that you engrave with their specific information.

Pet Toys Business

Designing, manufacturing, and wholesaling pet toys could put you on the path to financial freedom. The toys can be sold on a wholesale basis to pet retailers, or even directly to consumers through the internet and mail order.

Pet Travel Service Provider

Many people travel with their pets. Sometimes it is a stressful experience. You can offer a service that helps pet owners transport their pets.

Pets Training Business

Pets training is a must for every pet. Every pet owners look for good quality training providers.

Knowledge and skill are a must. You can start the business from home.

Pooper Scooper Service

This is an easy business to start. It requires little investment, no special skills, and minimal equipment to operate. A local newspaper advertisement is the best way to promote this service.

Publishing Pet Magazines

Publishing pet magazines is a very profitable business. Information is the key aspect. The advertisement revenue potential is very lucrative.

Tropical Fish Selling Business

The tropical fish market is huge globally. The profit margin is also very high. The fishes can be sold on a wholesale basis or by individual aquarium owners.

Bird's Selling

Bird's selling business has a huge market potential worldwide. Put your emphasis on the collection of different types of birds. Colorful birds are the most attractive pets.

Veterinary Clinic

One of the most profitable pet-related business ideas for pet physicians. Start the clinic from home. Sell medicine for extra earnings.

Arranging Dog Show

Dog shows are very adorable entertainment for pet lovers. Pet owners also love to participate in this type of function. You can also earn advertising revenue from the event.

Frequently Asked Questions on Pet Business

How do I start a pet business?

For beginners, it is essential to understand the local pet industry and the needs of the pet owners before jumping into starting a pet business. Some of the steps one should follow are the following;

- Understand the local market
- Select a niche
- Create a business plan
- Find a proper location
- Register your business
- Get licenses and permits
- Arrange finance, if required
- Have a marketing plan on where and how to sell.

What pet products sell best?

Some of the pet products that are selling best are pet toys, pet cages, pet clothes, novelty pet beds, and pet litter mats.

How does the pet industry make money?

The most popular ways of making money in the pet business are either by providing services to pet owners or create a product that helps in managing a pet.

Is the pet industry growing?

Yes, the pet industry is growing in almost all countries worldwide. For example, in the United States alone, pet market sales have grown from $51 billion in 2011 to an estimated $99 billion in the last year.

Benefits of Using Pet Sitting Service

When you decide to keep a pet, you should already have a plan on how you are going to take care of it. Just like humans, pets also need to be given good care and they should receive attention from their owners. This way, you will get to bond with your pet on different levels.

Taking care of pets does not mean giving them food and a nice place to sleep on. It entails a lot of things. Spending time with them, taking them for a walk, and taking them to a veterinary clinic for checkups are among the things you should be ready to do when you decide to keep a pet.

There are also some instances where you can be forced to use professional pet sitting services. When you go on vacation since you want to take a break from your job. Or, when you are taking your lady on a cruise that doesn't have any plans for pets.

Well, some people would often hire their neighbor's kid to watch over the pets when they are gone. This isn't the best thing to do. Most often, teens are considered to be less reliable. Not only will your pets be in unsafe hands, but your house as well, will be at great risk and vulnerable to various types of accidents.

You can also check out QC pet sitting in Raleigh NC for more information. With that said, let us look at a few benefits you can get from using pet sitting services.

Pet care

Benefits of Using Pet Sitting Service, taking good care of your pets entails a lot of things. Some of these things cannot be accomplished when you leave your animals in the hands of an untrained teenager.

When you hire a professional sitter, he or she will do more than just feed your cat or dog. They will make sure your dog gets enough exercise on a regular basis. They are also trained on various pet medications.

This means they can give the animals medical attention when needed. They also know the right diet to give your cat or dog when you are away. This will make your pet grow healthy.

Customized needs

Well, when you hire a teenager, all they will do is watch over your cat or dog and give it any food they'll find around. The way they take care of pets is the same in all houses regardless of how they are designed.

As we know, each pet and home is always unique. With professional sitting services, you will get customized care that is tailored towards your needs and that of your pets.

You can always be sure of great pet sitting services since professional sitters always follow specific instructions for various types of homes and pet care.

Convenience

If you choose to have your neighbor's kid to watch over your dog when you are gone, you will need to take the dog to your neighbor's house. Otherwise, when they come to get it, you might be forced to pay a lot. However, when you find a good pet sitting service, you won't need to worry about transporting your dog or cat. Also, you can get agencies that offer home care as well. This way, you will be getting two services done professionally at a fair price.

Pet safety

As mentioned before, your pets should continue to be safe even when you are not around. You should ensure that your pets will continue to be loved and will remain healthy till you come back. This is why you need well trained sitters.

For instance, when your cat gets into an accident, the pet sitter will rush it to the clinic. You should however try to find out if the agency will let you fill a vet release form. This is what will make your cat get treatment from the vet in your absence.

Leaving your pets in the hands of a professional sitter ensures that your cat stays safe. This will give you peace of mind and let you enjoy your vacation like you are supposed to.

Difference between a Professional Pet Sitter and a Hobby Pet Sitter

Finding a pet sitter online through platforms like Rover can be much like finding a ride through Uber or lodging through Airbnb. Most of the people offering their services through these platforms are not full-time taxi drivers or hotel managers, or pet sitters. However, even if it's a side job, they can still still be very good at it.

However, if you're extra cautious, have animals with special needs, or simply like to prepare for any eventuality, you should look for a professional pet sitter instead of a friendly stranger.

According to Pet Sitters International (PSI), a national educational association for professional pet sitters, professional pet sitters will:

Have a local business license, if required

Are insured and bonded in case of injuries or damages to your pet, themselves, their own pets, personal property and/or third parties

Asks clients to sign a contract

Has pet-care training and certifications for first aid and CPR, for example

Is certified by a professional association such as PSI or the National Association of Pet Sitters (NAPPS).

Offers pet sitting or walking as their primary business

Professional Pet Sitters

Professional pet sitters may also have additional certifications from other organizations such as the National Dog Groomers Association (NDGAA), International Boarding and Pet Services Association (IBPSA), Certification Council for Professional Dog Trainers (CCPDT) or the Professional Animal Care Certification Council (PACCC).

Some part-time pet sitters may have insurance and professional certifications themselves, even if they only work at their leisure. Therefore, it's important to interview potential pet sitters, professional or not, before officially booking their services.

Always Interview Potential Pet Sitters

Whichever pet care professional you're looking for "sitter, walker, groomer or boarding service" they all require the same level of screening. Word of mouth, or customer reviews if you're searching online, are definitely helpful. But, you should interview your soon-to-be pet care professional yourself" in person and with your pet present—to make sure they can meet both you and your pet's specific needs.

Pet Sitters International recommends that you:

Ask the sitter if they have a business license to offer their services in your city or state. Pet sitters who are self-employed and do it as a hobby, as is the case with many sitters found online, probably don't need one. Now, if the pet sitter works for or owns an established business that offers other pet care services, said business should have up-to-date authorization.

- Make sure the pet sitter is insured and bonded and ask for proof of coverage.

- Ask for proof of clean criminal history.

- Ask for a client reference list you can contact and carefully check written reviews from previous customers.

- Consider whether the sitter is a member of a pet care association where they have access to educational resources or training courses.

- If you're hiring through a pet-sitting service, ask whether they screen or train their employees.

- **Pay attention to the details**: how long does the sitter takes to respond to your inquiries, how much notice they need before scheduling their services, what are their service costs, how much time they'll spend with your pet, do they require a deposit, and/or if the sitter has an emergency plan for medical or natural emergencies.

Where Can I Find a Certified Professional Pet Sitter?

Pet Sitters International (PSI)

PSI is an education association for professional pet sitters. They offer their members a Certified Professional Pet Sitter (CPPS) certification which they state is "the industry only knowledge-assessed certification exam for professional pet sitters.

To receive the certification, sitters are tested for their knowledge about:

- General pet sitting
- Specific care of dogs, cats, and pet birds
- Animal first aid and health
- Parasites and sanitation

- Pet-sitter health and safety
- Client interviews and customer service

- Disaster planning
- Legal issues and pet-sitter liability

The PSI also offers additional online courses for Professional Pet Sitting as a Career.

You can find a PSI certified pet sitter through their Find a Local PSI Pet Sitter tool. You can search by zip code and type of pet (dog, cat, fish, bird, reptiles and amphibians, horses, farm animals, exotic pets, caged pets and special needs pets).

National Association of Professional Pet Sitters (NAPPS)

NAPPS is a non-profit association that supports members with certifications and educational resources to operate successful pet sitting businesses.

Their certification course covers topics such as pet care and safety, health, nutrition and behavior for a variety of animals. It also includes a first aid course and business development and management.

Members can get other certifications for feline behavioral issues, canine body language, and care for parrots, senior dogs, toy dogs, and horses.

To find a NAPPS certified sitter use the Local NAPPS Pet Sitter tool.

Benefits of Pet Sitting Over Pet Boarding

Pet boarding facilities, or pet hotels, are another option when planning a long trip. Yet, time away from you and their home can be very stressful for pets.

In some of these facilities, pets could spend most of their time locked in kennels or cages, lacking necessary exercise and attention. As a result, your pet may refuse to eat, have high levels of anxiety, or even become sick. In fact, vets recommend watching out for symptoms of kennel cough, diarrhea, lethargy, and any changes in eating patterns once your pet returns home.

According to the NAPPS, leaving your pets at home under the care of a sitter can reduce their stress levels as they'll be in their familiar environment without new scents or sounds that can overwhelm them. Their daily routine could remain mostly unchanged if you find a sitter who can follow detailed instructions for walking routes, potty breaks, and eating or play times. Not to mention you eliminate your pet's risk of catching any unwanted illness from other pets.

Hiring the same pet sitter long-term can also reduce the chances of your pet experiencing separation anxiety. According to the American Society for the Prevention of Cruelty to Animals (ASPCA), separation anxiety is one of the most common complaints of pet parents is that their dogs are disruptive or destructive when left alone. Separation anxiety may cause behavioral issues such as urinating and defecating out of their scheduled times, coprophagia (eating their own excrement), barking and howling excessively, destroying household items, escaping, or constant pacing.

Pet Sitting Insurance Policy Information

Pet Sitting Insurance

Pet Sitting Insurance. If you're a pet sitter, business insurance is a smart purchase. The pet industry has never been hotter than it is now. Although many families or individuals in times past often acquired new pets without a lot of forethought, people today take pet ownership more seriously, often putting a lot of thought into selecting a pet and caring for it.

With this has come the advent of pet services for these pets, including pet sitters who provide alternatives for pet owners when they must be away from home on vacation or traveling for business. Pet sitters are a wonderful alternative to kennels in some instances, and pet sitters are in high demand. Before taking on your first clients, protect yourself and your business with pet sitting insurance.

Pet sitters services generally include feeding, exercise runs, and grooming. "Doggie day cares" allow owners to place their dogs at the kennel or pet sitters home during the day and pick them up after work.

Pet sitting insurance protects your business from lawsuits with rates as low as $27/mo. Get a fast quote and your certificate of insurance now.

Below are some answers to commonly asked pet sitting insurance questions:

- How Much Does Pet Sitting Insurance Cost?
- Why Buy Pet Sitting Insurance?
- Who Should Buy Pet Sitting Insurance?
- What Are Some Pet Sitting Insurance Claims Examples?

- What Does Insurance For Pet Sitters Cover??

- How Much Does Pet Sitting Insurance Cost?

The average price of a standard $1,000,000/$2,000,000 General Liability Insurance policy for small pet sitting businesses ranges from $27 to $39 per month based on location, size, payroll, sales and experience.

Why Buy Pet Sitting Insurance?

Americans spend hundreds of dollars each year on their pets, with spending on pets amounting to more than spending on men's apparel. As a nation, pet owners spend around $50 billion each year on pets and pet care. According to Pet Sitters International, pet sitters sat with pets on 18.5 million occasions in 2010, which was up nearly 1 million visit when compared to 2007 levels. Revenues from members of Pet Sitters International in 2010 were in excess of $325 million.

More households have dogs than have children: around 43 million U.S. households have dogs. Around 84 percent of the organization's members have bonding and liability insurance. This mean a large risk exposure with such a busy industry.

Who Should Buy Pet Sitting Insurance?

Pet Sitter Cleaning Up Dog Poop

Pet sitters should consider pet sitting insurance. If you care for or feed pets for a living, including dogs, cats, birds, reptiles, and fish or if you provide doggy day care or dog boarding in your home, it is an essential purchase as part of doing business. If you sit in a client's home or provide live-in pet sitting services for clients while they travel, it is also a necessity.

Other professions, such as pet groomers, dog trainers, pet taxi service professionals, or those providing home security services to make the home look as if it is occupied while someone is away are also candidates for pet sitting insurance.

The insurance you select should cover all of the perils possible in the profession, which means that you are not left holding the bag when a vet bill, lawsuit, or claim against you occurs. Essentially, you need to protect yourself from anything that might happen to the animal or the client's property while you are working.

When you purchase a policy, be sure to read it thoroughly to ensure that you have no gasps in coverage or exclusions to contend with. Work with an agent who is seasoned in the pet insurance niche and specialty insurance policies to find the right type of policy for your individual needs.

What Are Some Pet Sitting Insurance Claims Examples?

Consider all the risks that your business is under when you are looking for pet sitting insurance coverage. This will help you find a policy that provides adequate insurance for you. Work with your agent to create a tailor-made policy that covers your potential perils and you'll have peace of mind with your purchase - and be protected from liability and financial harm.

Some of the types of claims scenarios that you might want to consider before making a purchase include:

- If a pet is harmed accidentally or becomes sick while you're caring for it, who is responsible?
- What occurs is a pet in your care is stolen?

- What happens if a pet reacts poorly to a pet grooming product and needs veterinary care?
- Who pays the bill if a pet needs to see the vet while you're sitting it?
- If something comes up missing while you're sitting in a client's home, what happens?
- If you cause a fire in a client's home, who is responsible?
- If you break something of value in a client's home, who pays for replacement?

These are most of the potential claims cenarios for pet sitters. Discussing scenarios such as these with your agent can help ensure that you get a pet sitting insurance policy that meets your particular needs and addresses your concerns.

What Does Pet Sitting Insurance Cover?

A typical insurance policy for pet sitters covers many of the same areas that other business insurance covers. There is a loss potential any time a business owner cares for the belongings of others, including pets. Coverage usually includes:

Pet sitting liability insurance. This is a type of coverage that provides protection for you as a pet sitter if you are found to be at fault for property damage or injury to a pet during the course of your work. This may include things like medical expenses for injured pets, damage from fire due to your negligence, or lost keys.

Control, custody, and care of pet insurance. This type of policy provides protection for accidents that may occur when you are in control of, have custody of, or are caring for pets. Limits may range from $10K to $200K for each type of covered event.

Pet transportation insurance. Sometimes referred to as pet taxi insurance, this type of insurance cover you for pet transport while you haul a pet while on the job.

Pet Sitter's Risks & Exposures

Pet Sitter Holding Dog

Premises liability exposure Leashes and carriers should be required to protect customers and other animals. Veterinary records confirming appropriate inoculations should be required of any animal being boarded to prevent the spread of disease. Enclosures should be secured to prevent escape, with each animal boarded separately to prevent attacks by other animals.

Escaped animals could attack people or other animals, or cause damage to neighboring properties. Daytime open kenneling can result in serious injuries. Precautions such as temperament testing, adequate staff monitoring, requiring participating dogs to be spayed or neutered and divided play areas by the size of dog are helpful.

Products liability exposure is moderate if the pet sitter sells animal food and supplies. The exposure increases to that of a manufacturer if the sitter modifies or sells a directly imported product.

Environmental impairment exposure is moderate due to the potential for air, surface or ground water, or soil contamination from the handling and disposal of biological waste material. The pet sitter must follow all federal and state procedures for disposal.

Workers compensation exposure is high due to the unpredictability of even the most domesticated animal. Workers may be injured by biting, scratching, kicking, or other attack. All employees must be trained in appropriate restraint techniques. Problem animals should be clearly identified so that appropriate precautions can be taken.

Other common injuries include lifting that results in back strains or sprains, trips and falls, respiratory ailments from inhaling dander, and communicable diseases transmitted by animals. Special training in separating fighting dogs is required in facilities where daytime kenneling occurs.

Property exposure includes an office and boarding facilities for animals. Ignition sources include electrical wiring, heating, and air conditioning.

There may be laundry equipment used to clean bedding which can overheat. All should be well maintained and meet current codes. Food and bedding supplies are combustible and should be stored away from heat sources. Poor housekeeping is a serious fire hazard. Animals may be a target for theft or vandalism.

All enclosures must be properly secured. Controls should be in place to prevent access to the premises after hours. Alarms are recommended.

Crime exposure is from employee dishonesty. Background checks should be conducted on all employees handling money.

Inland marine exposure is from accounts receivable for credit customers, bailees customers for animals boarded, and valuable papers and records for customers' and suppliers' information. There may be computers used for recordkeeping.

Business auto exposure is generally limited to hired and non-owned for employees running errands. If the kennel provides pickup or delivery services, all drivers must be licensed with acceptable MVRs. All vehicles must be well maintained with documentation kept in a central location.

Commercial Insurance And Business Industry Classification

SIC CODE: 0752 Animal Specialty Services, Except Veterinary

NAICS CODE: 812910 Pet Care (except Veterinary) Services

Suggested ISO General Liability Code(s): 16404

Description for 0752: Animal Specialty Services, Except Veterinary

Division A: Agriculture, Forestry, And Fishing | Major Group 07: Agricultural Services | Industry Group 075: Animal Services, Except Veterinary

0752 Animal Specialty Services, Except Veterinary: Establishments primarily engaged in performing services, except veterinary, for pets, equines, and other animal specialties.

Animal shelters

Artificial insemination services: animal specialties

Boarding horses

Boarding kennels

Breeding of animals, other than cattle hogs, sheep, goats, and poultry

Dog grooming

Dog pounds

Honey straining on the farm

Pedigree record services for pets and other animal specialties

Showing of pets and other animal specialties

Training horses, except racing

Training of pets and other animal specialties

Vaccinating pets and other animal specialties, except by veterinarians

www.ingramcontent.com/pod-product-compliance
Lightning Source LLC
Chambersburg PA
CBHW070202230526
45471CB00002B/775